# MY Gratitude Sou... Your Own

(A note to grown ups who might be a helping a child with this activity book: Encourage your child to draw themselves as their favorite pretend character/alter ego, to help having gratitude be more fun and gratifying for them. Also, consider using photos, cut outs from newspapers or magazines, spare buttons, ribbon, or anything else you have around the house to make collages in your child's Gratitude Soup book, adding texture and visual stimulation.)

by YOU

Gratitude Soup Create Your Own, copyright 2010, all rights reserved. A Self Publication, 2118 Wilshire Boulevard, Suite 108, Santa Monica, California, 90403.

ISBN 1492707570

EAN-13 9781492707578

Draw a picture of yourself feeling happy.
When do you feel the most happiness?

Hi! I'm

———————————————————————————,

And this is my story of gratitude,

And how it changed my feelings inside, and my attitude.

You see, usually I was ready to be silly,

Easily, breezily, ready to be willy nilly,

Giggles funning,

Smiles bouncing, jumping, running,

Happiness could flow you know

How do you look when you have a strong case of the Gimme Gimme Wants Wants? Do you feel anger? Sadness? Frustration? Draw or paste a photo your face when have those feelings in you.

Except that sometimes
I caught a case
Of the gimme, gimme want wants,
I became a cranky one,
Almost undone and not much fun,
And on my face not a trace
of that happier space.
I screamed on the inside,
"I need more toys!"
I screamed to the outside,
"I need more toys!"
But Mommy and Daddy didn't give me toys
When I lost my poise
And made all that noise.
So I yelled louder, "I want more!"
But still no toys, what a bore.
My parents knew in their core
I didn't need more.
But their poor child
They couldn't just ignore.
Mommy said sweetly,
"It's not toys that you need,
Indeed, there's something better--
It's your soul we'll feed.
I know just where to start,
We'll make Gratitude Soup
In your heart."

I know how
And we can make some right now.
Here's how you do it,
There's nearly nothing to it.
All you need is not a lot:
An imaginary spoon
And a pot.  That I've got!
And then search your mind, rewind:
See if you can find…

All that you love and like,
Like…

_____

_____

_____

_____

I, _____,
Looooooooooove to cook,
And I know just where to look
To make perfect Gratitude Soup.
It's so fun, I like to start it with a
"Whoopity whoop!"

These 2 pages are for you to draw or make a collage of anything that you love, like, and appreciate.

Create yourself adding ingredients to your soup. What are some of your favorite experiences? What will you put in your Gratitude Soup?

One by one, I put them in the pot.
My, my! I can think of a lot!
The more I find I have Gratitude for,
The more I find I have to adore!
So I search myself to my core,
And I find I am grateful for even more!

I am grateful _____

_____

I am grateful _____

_____

The more I think about my gratitude,
The happier and happier is my attitude!
Changing my focus is like hocus pocus;
My heart lightens, my feeling brightens!

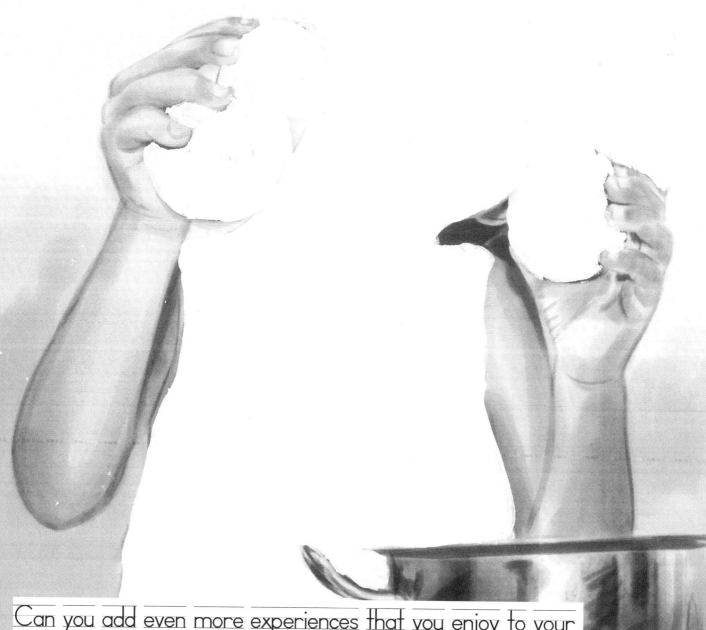

Can you add even more experiences that you enjoy to your Gratitude Soup? What kind of feeling do these experiences bring out of you?

Thoughts of gratitude
Keep on coming through,
So I keep singing and cooking.
What can I do?  Wouldn't you?
I can tell I'm not through
When my happiness grows and grows,
And the joy in my smile shows
I have even more gratitude
Ready for cooking.
Gratitude can show up
When you're not even looking!


I am grateful _____

_____

_____

I am grateful _____

_____

_____

Draw or paste a picture of your serious look when you are feeling your gratitude.

Now this is the serious part.
It's so serious,
I almost don't know where to start.
Feel all of your gratitude alive in your heart,
Flowing and growing,
Knowing the beauty of this gratitude art.

How do you look when you are feeling tender loving care? Can you draw or paste a picture of yourself stirring your gratitude soup with tender loving care?

Then watch the swirl
And whirl,
The curls unfurl,
As you stir
All that you're grateful for,
All that you adore,
Your gratitude growing more and more.
Can you feel your heart soar?

You can add some love in there,
And even tender loving care
If you're aware
That you have some to spare.

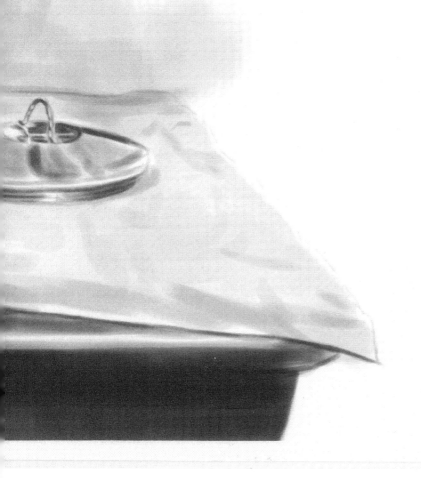

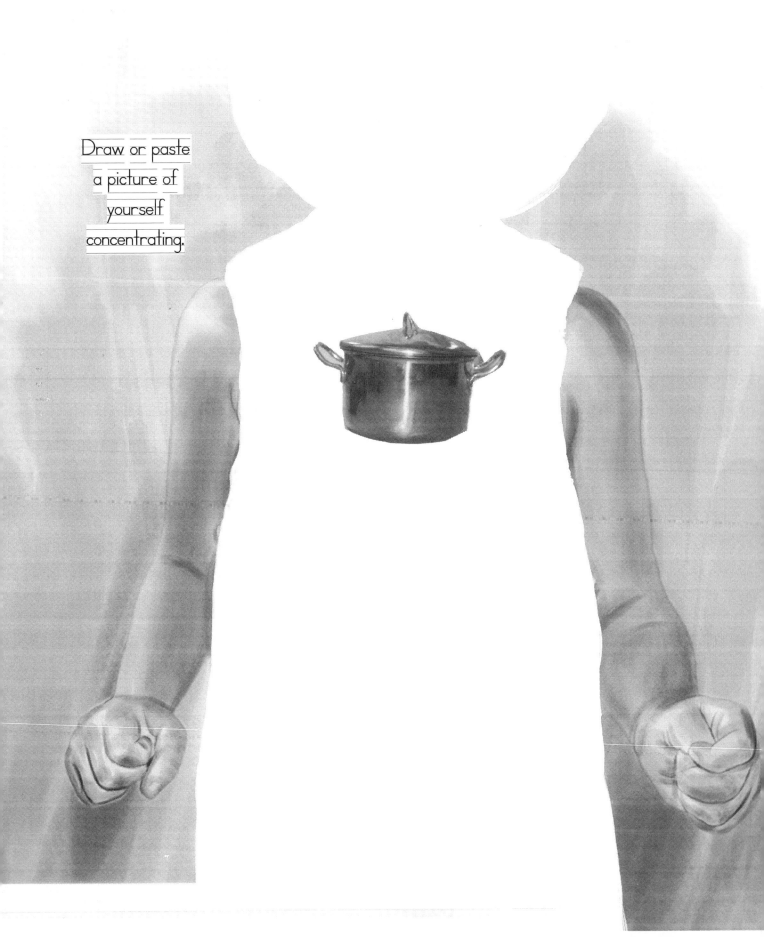

Draw or paste
a picture of
yourself
concentrating.

Concentrate a lot,
You can do it with your thought,
Yes, give it all you've got,
And shrink the imaginary pot
So that in your heart it fits,
And there it sits, as good as goodness gets.
With your love, keep it warm
Every eve and every morn.

You can sip Gratitude Soup all day,
And you can sip Gratitude Soup all night,
Gratitude makes the best soup, I say,
Filling me with love and light.

And it's just right there,
Ready to share, ready to care,
In my heart, ready to exude,
And feed my soul with gratitude.

Draw or paste a picture of yourself feeling of full of love, appreciation, and your delicious Gratitude Soup.

And that's how I,

_____,

became

_____.

Gratitude Soup helps me love even more
All the experiences I already adore.
Try some yourself and see what it's for.

You can make it any time, any day,
It's not hard work--it's more like play.
Start cooking, okay?  What do you say?
Feed your soul with gratitude and
You, too, will say, "Yay!  Hip hip hooray!"

# Gratitude Soup

Olivia Rosewood

# Gratitude Soup Create Your Own

by YOU
& Olivia Rosewood

# Brave Enough to Bloom

By Olivia Rosewood

# The Book of Gold

by Olivia Rosewood

# Dimitry and the Moon

By Olivia Rosewood

Beatrice is a Butterfly ...
for Now

Olivia Rosewood

# Clia
## The First Bird Ever

Based on the true story.

By Olivia Rosewood